CAN YOU BE HAPPY for 100 DAYS IN a ROW?

CAN YOU BE HAPPY for 100 DAYS IN a ROW?

DMITRY GOLUBNICHY

ARTISAN | NEW YORK

Names: Golubnichy, Dmitry, author.
Title: Can you be happy for 100 days in a row?/Dmitry Golubnichy.
Description: New York City : Artisan, a division of Workman Publishing Co., Inc. [2017].
Identifiers: LCCN 2017000365 | ISBN 9781579657154 (pbk.)
Subjects: LCSH: Happiness. | Contentment. | Colors—Miscellanea.
Classification: LCC BJ1481 .G623 2017 | DDC 158—dc23 LC record available
at https://lccn.loc.gov/2017000365

Text by Elland Road Partners
Interior illustrations and lettering by Timothy Goodman and John Sampson
Cover design and illustrations by Timothy Goodman
Art direction by Michelle Ishay-Cohen
Design by Renata Di Biase

Artisan books are available at special discounts when purchased in bulk for premiums
and sales promotions as well as for fund-raising or educational use. Special editions or
book excerpts also can be created to specification. For details, contact the Special Sales
Director at the address below, or send an e-mail to specialmarkets@workman.com.

Published by Artisan
A division of Workman Publishing Co., Inc.
225 Varick Street
New York, NY 10014-4381
artisanbooks.com

Artisan is a registered trademark of Workman Publishing Co., Inc.

Published simultaneously in Canada by Thomas Allen & Son, Limited

Printed in China

First printing, November 2017

1 3 5 7 9 10 8 6 4 2

To everyone who has taken on the #100HappyDays challenge and to those who are about to do so

CONTENTS

INTRODUCTION

Hi. I'm Dmitry, the creator of the #100HappyDays challenge.

When I started the challenge, I already had everything that was supposed to make me happy: a dream job in the education sector with a good salary, passport stamps from more than fifty countries, an attic apartment in the heart of Zurich, a lovely girlfriend by my side. I was living the life. But even with all those boxes checked off, I still didn't feel satisfied. I felt like I needed to chase more, new, better . . .

So I took a trip back home to Riga, Latvia, where most of my childhood friends had settled. And I noticed something: They were very content working the same jobs they'd had since high school, living in their small apartments, marrying their childhood sweethearts, going for weekly beers with buddies. They didn't care about finding the fanciest club or the most beautiful seashore. Rather than flying off to Polynesia or the Amalfi Coast, they were happily honeymooning in a small town fifty kilometers (thirty miles) from Riga where there is—trust me on this—literally nothing to do. Me? I was miserable about the lack of really great snow in the Swiss Alps during that skiing season.

Clearly, my unhappiness was coming from within. I needed a new perspective. Just as I had set about achieving ambitious career goals, I decided that discovering what makes me happy would be my priority for the next hundred days. And to hold myself accountable, I promised to post a photo of my findings daily on social media with the hashtag #100HappyDays.

Around day 12, people began asking what I was up to. Our exchanges often went like this: *What are you doing?* Appreciating what makes me happy. *Can I join?* Of course! *What are the rules?* Just find what makes you happy, post about it, and repeat for 100 days!

Soon friends of friends wanted to do their own happiness challenge and asked me to create a website to answer their questions. On December 30, 2014, 100HappyDays.com went live, and that same day, three thousand people registered. I realized this was bigger than my own happiness quest.

But what did I learn about what makes me happy?

- Happiness is an active choice.
- Happiness lies in small things.

- Happiness is most real when it's shared with others.
- To achieve happiness, it helps to appreciate and accept uncertainty.

Before long, I grew less concerned with my own mental state and more interested in helping others discover their personal happiness. And it turns out that I am happier when I am empowering others to focus on joy!

To date, more than 8 million people worldwide have taken on the #100HappyDays challenge, celebrating over 25 million happy moments. Participants are randomly selected to rate their happiness levels on days 1, 25, 50, 75, and 100. By the end of the challenge, people report being an average of 19 percent happier than when they started it! Participants say the challenge helps them notice what makes them happy. It improves their mood and makes them appreciate their life. They become more optimistic, they receive more compliments, and they realize how fortunate they are—they even fall in love!

As for me, I now work full-time with the 100 Happy Days Foundation to inspire people to choose a happier existence. And I wrote this book to help you do just that.

HOW TO USE THIS BOOK

So how do you do your own #100HappyDays challenge? Find something that makes you happy every day for a hundred days. It's as simple as that.

Many people start and stop the challenge, citing not enough time as the reason. This book is meant to help you make it through by supplying ideas and inspiration. On the following pages, you will find a hundred happiness-inducing suggestions inspired by doing the challenge myself, watching others, and reading and thinking about happiness full-time.

Please remember, though, that this is *your* happiness journey, and you should customize it as you wish. If riding your bike really fast (Day 16) isn't your thing, move on to something that is. And if decluttering a drawer (Day 88) will bring you joy two or three days in a row, that counts too. You can choose to open to a random spot every day or proceed page by page.

Throughout the book, you'll also find Science of Happiness essays that go deeper into the research-based findings on what tends to make us happy, so that you can better understand why self-care, physical activity, and connecting to nature, for example, are essential to achieving lasting happiness.

It helps to create support for your happiness challenge. Pick your favorite social network and share photos of your happiness journey there using the hashtag #100HappyDaysBook, or you can simply send your pictures to MyHappyDay@100HappyDays.com to do it privately.

The most important thing to remember is that this is for you and no one else—you don't have to compete with anyone else's happiness levels, and it won't make you happier to cheat. Discovering what makes you happy is its own success!

And now you're ready to become an expert on your own happiness. Off you go!

GET LOST IN A PAINTING

Day 1

Wander a nearby gallery or museum in search of a piece that sets your heart aflutter. A Matisse might do the trick, but so too could an obscure impressionistic work or a postmodern statement (one of my favorite paintings is *Yellow-Red-Blue* by Wassily Kandinsky). Don't worry about appreciating the movement of the brushstrokes or an interesting composition. Just relish the joy of the discovery process and give yourself the space to admire something that speaks to your soul.

GO THE EXTRA MILE

Bring a friend along. Once you've each spent time admiring a piece, take turns sharing your perspective. It will deepen your enjoyment of the day, and your friendship.

Day 2

*"In every walk with nature, one
 receives far more than he seeks."*
—John Muir

A Stanford study found that walking in
nature for ninety minutes can ward off
negative thoughts and reduce a person's
risk of developing mental illness. That's
because natural environments have a
restorative and relaxing effect on the
brain. Plus, trekking in the daytime
gets you out in the sunshine, which
stimulates the brain chemicals that
improve mood. Enough talk. Go take
a hike!

CLIMB

Fresh

INTO
SHEETS

BRING @ CO-WORKER COFFEE

Day 4

Kindness is contagious—it creates a better environment for everyone. And it has some self-serving benefits as well, especially in the workplace: Your most thoughtful colleagues are not only more committed and less likely to quit their jobs, they are also the happiest. A University of Wisconsin study found that office altruists got an immediate psychological reward from helping others and were also more satisfied with their life thirty years later. So do yourself a favor and surprise an associate with a latte today.

KEEP IT GOING

Visit 100HappyDays .org/KindnessNinja .me (a project from the 100 Happy Days Foundation) for the world's biggest kindness scavenger hunt.

Day 5

Chocolate has several ingredients that work happy-making magic on our brains—trimethylxanthine, theobromine, tryptophan, serotonin, and anandamide, to name a few. And, it's delicious! So while you wait for the wonder chemicals to take effect, savor every moment of the experience: the snap of your first piece, the smell, the taste, the melt-in-your-mouth feeling, and, of course, the moment you go back for another bite.

WRITE DOW
THINGS YO
Grateful

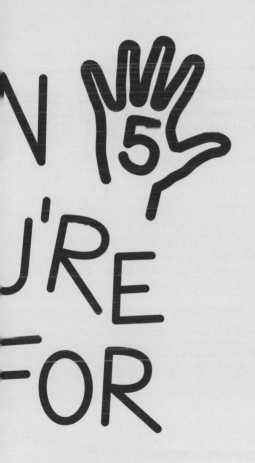

Day 6

What do you appreciate in your life at this very moment? A walk on a sunny afternoon? A calm moment with your child? Cultivating gratitude alters your psyche, whatever the source of your appreciation, leading to greater optimism, joy, generosity, compassion, and forgiveness; a stronger immune system; and a better night's sleep. All the more reason to feel grateful!

KEEP IT GOING

Start a nightly gratitude journal: Before drifting off to sleep, jot down the moments from each day that made you thankful.

CHOOSE EXPERIENCES OVER THINGS

It's not completely true that money can't buy happiness. Sometimes it can, and we know this from a branch of science known as "positive psychology," which is essentially the study of what makes people happy. First, people with little or no money are definitely happier when they can afford the basics: food, shelter, health care. Money also brings joy when we give some of ours to others (see page 42). But there is another way that money can be uplifting, and it explains much about the happiness journey: People who spend on experiences—vacations, dance lessons, restaurant meals, sporting events—are often happier than people who mostly buy things. This might seem counter-intuitive, as cars and computers stay around longer. But humans quickly lose interest in material pleasures—that new car smell fades fast—while experiences endure in the memories we cherish, in the anecdotes we tell, and in the ways they inform our sense of who we are.

In part, that's because we tend to evaluate experiences on their own terms but compare possessions to what others have. Research has shown that if a person buys a car and his friend buys a fancier model, he may well be envious. But if he returns from a vacation to learn that a friend stayed in a nicer hotel on hers, he will be less bothered because he still has his unique memories.

Throughout this book, you will be urged to try new experiences. Remember: The joy in most journeys is in the trip itself.

BE A
Tourist
in YOUR
OWN
CITY

Day 7

Your destination today: the must-see spot where you send all of your out-of-town visitors. Go on a tour with an expert, get tickets to a big attraction, take advantage of cliché photo ops, or book a night in a hotel. It's a passport to a new perspective on your hometown—and the places in it that bring you joy.

Day 8

The benefits of a lovely home aren't just aesthetic. Physical environments also can have a profound effect on mood: Bright colors help us feel more alive, earth tones soothe, and leafy plants increase creativity. Practitioners of the Chinese philosophy of feng shui harmonize their homes by directing the flow of water and wind (the energies that make up our life force, or chi) for optimal living. Follow their lead and start in your bedroom, where it matters most. Move your bed to the commanding position: the spot farthest from the door that still has a full view of the door and the room. According to the principles of feng shui, waking up in this safe, strong position will help you feel calmer and more secure in your home.

RE-ARRANGE THE FURNITURE

Day 10

Soap bubbles are a symbol of childhood joy. They remind us that happiness is found in the smallest elements of daily life—just a few bubbles away. This simple notion inspired the annual Global Bubble Parade, organized by our 100 Happy Days Foundation. In cities around the world, passionate individuals gather to do just what the name suggests—create a parade of bubble blowers united in the belief that happiness is the journey, not the destination. Today, break out a wand and create a delightful moment of your own.

GO THE EXTRA MILE

For a fresh perspective and a moment of glee, blow bubbles at night or in freezing temperatures.

Day 11

Connecting someone you cherish with another friend is a lovely way to make your happiness journey a group trip. So strengthen your social circle today by inviting people with shared interests over for dinner or typing "You two should meet" in the subject header on an e-mail to folks who you know will enjoy grabbing coffee or a drink (with or without you).

Day 12

Whether on your own at home or at the club, it's time to blast the music and listen for the beat. For as long as humans have roamed the earth, they have danced in worship and celebration, for entertainment and to achieve an ecstatic trance—from hunter-gatherers' ritualized movements to the wild rumpus of Dionysus's followers to today's twerkers. And for good reason: Moving to the rhythm connects us with ourselves and our community and also minimizes stress hormones and sparks joyful ones.

HUGitO

Day 13

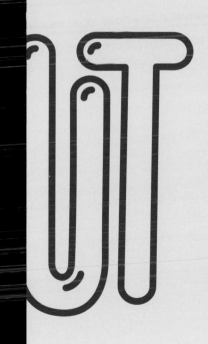

More than 32 million people have waited in line, sometimes for hours, for a brief embrace from Amma (aka Mother), the Hindu "hugging saint" whose arms have consoled the suffering for nearly fifty years. And research shows that she's onto something: A big squeeze has powerful effects—one study found that athletes who hug their teammates play better. Hugs also protect us from stress-induced sickness, never mind the germs. When we embrace, the pressure on our skin sends calming signals to the vagus nerve, which slows down heart rate. Hugs also decrease the release of cortisol, which makes us feel stressed, and increase the release of oxytocin, which makes us happy. Ultimately, though, what we crave and what we get is connection.

LENDING A HAND

Research across the social sciences has demonstrated that humans are quicker than any other species to assist those in need, strangers included. Indeed, we are hardwired to help: fMRI technology has shown that giving to others stimulates the same parts of the brain that eating and having sex do!

The reason our instincts for generosity, empathy, and cooperation have evolved is that these qualities make the groups we belong to stronger, and thus more likely to survive. If that sounds selfish, it is no cause for shame. It's like that old saying *I'll scratch your back if you scratch mine*. We experience altruism positively—we are happier when we are helping—because it encourages more of the same behavior, creating a feedback loop that binds humans to one another. That is itself a happy-making circumstance (see page 90).

Of course, altruism makes the individual stronger too. Helping others diverts our attention away from ourselves and our personal problems, lessening their importance by highlighting our relative advantage. In any case, doing something for someone else is always worth the effort because inevitably you'll be a beneficiary too.

DONATE

Day 14

Lightening your load and helping
someone in need is a double dose
of positive vibes. You'll benefit
from streamlining your home—
good for reducing stress and feeling
empowered—and donating to a worthy
cause, which activates your dopamine
reward pathway (the same part of the
brain that's turned on when you smooch
a lover or eat a chocolate-chip cookie).

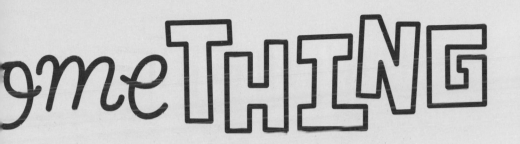

WAYS TO DONATE

- **DONATION TOWN** (DonationTown .org) connects donators to local charities that accept clothes and household items.
- **GOODWILL INDUSTRIES** (Goodwill.org) accepts all manner of goods at their stores and in donation boxes.
- **HABITAT FOR HUMANITY RESTORES** (Habitat.org/ Restores) are great places to donate new and gently used appliances, furniture, building materials, and household goods.

- **MR. HOLLAND'S OPUS FOUNDATION** (MHOpus.org) refurbishes and donates used musical instruments to school music programs.
- **SPORTS GIFT** (SportsGift .org) distributes gently used equipment to underprivileged children in the United States.
- **THE FREECYCLE NETWORK** (Freecycle.org) allows you to post items you're ready to pass along.

MEMO-RIZE this POEM

Day 15

Or any poem that speaks to you and soothes your soul. It will speak to you in quiet or dark moments, acting as a doorway into the beauty and rhythm of life, a reminder of what is in your heart.

LET'S CHANGE FOR THE BETTER

Let's change for the better
into magical beings
and build new forevers
from all that we're seeing
and unhinge new futures
with all that we're breaking
let's change for the better
for the better we're making.
—Dallas Clayton

RIDE *yo*
REALLY

Day 17

Despite those warnings you got as a kid, chatting up strangers is a good idea—at least when it comes to your mood. In an experiment conducted with commuters, half talked to the passenger next to them; the others rode in solitude. Before the experiment began, the participants thought the ride would be better without these interactions, and that it would be hard to start conversations. They were wrong on both counts—the chattier bunch reported a more positive trip, and their exchanges flowed easily.

NOT SURE HOW TO START?

Seeking advice *"Do you know the best way to get to x?"* or finding common ground *"I loved that book"* is a good bet.

Day 18

Grab your feather duster, pump up the volume of your favorite guilty-pleasure tunes, and dust your way to mental clarity. The good-time feelings won't stop when you're through dusting—cleanliness brings balance, space to think and create, positive energy, and an overall sense of well-being.

Day 19

The sun really shines as a mood booster. When its rays hit your skin, your body produces vitamin D, which is magical for your frame of mind. Those rays also send a signal to your brain to produce more of the emotion-regulating chemical serotonin. It works like Prozac and other antidepressants, not to mention the high-intensity light boxes prescribed for people with seasonal affective disorder. So find a bench under the blue sky, lean back, and let the happy-making chemicals seep in.

Bask in the sun

Day 20

Longevity research has shown that lonely people don't live as long as their well-loved peers. Chalk it up to the fact that humans are, by nature, social creatures; those intimate relationships don't just feel warm and fuzzy, they also help regulate biological processes related to emotional and physical well-being. One of the best ways to relieve stress and promote healthy brain chemistry? Confiding in someone. Sharing your secrets with close friends is a great stress reliever, and has the added bonus of bringing you and your confidant closer together.

JOYFUL NOISE

There may be no better illustration of the mind-body connection than music's therapeutic effects. Scores of studies have shown that it improves both mood and physical health, and there's every reason to believe that a great deal of the first benefit is a result of the second. After all, who wouldn't feel happier if her blood pressure decreased and her heart rate slowed—which is exactly what happens when we listen to music.

Listening to music triggers positive responses not only in our autonomic nervous system, which controls circulation, but also in our limbic system, which is responsible for emotion and memory. So hearing music from an especially happy period of our lives can soothe body and soul by sparking recollections of past joy. Even sad music has been shown to lift spirits, maybe because we have a nonconscious awareness that the feelings will end when the music does.

Music's effect on happiness isn't limited to listening, though. Singing and playing in a group, for example, has been shown to make people happier, in part because the act of synchronizing increases one's sense of belonging (see page 90). Simply practicing an instrument seems to improve what neuroscientists call "executive function," the collection of brain processes that enables people to, among other things, solve problems, control behaviors, make good choices, and adjust to changing mental demands.

More than two thousand years ago, Plato, the classical Greek philosopher, wrote: "Musical training is a more potent instrument than any other, because rhythm and harmony find their way into the inward places of the soul, on which they mightily fasten, imparting grace, and making the soul of him who is rightly educated graceful." Turns out he was right.

CREATE an EXERCISE PLAYLIST

Day 21

Slip on some headphones and play DJ for your sweat session. Countless studies show that physical activity is one of the quickest routes to a happier you (see page 138) and that music can make the exertion feel less daunting—and improve the odds that you'll stick with it. So today, fuel your next endorphin high by crafting a killer, can't-wait-to-start-moving mix of upbeat, inspiring tunes. Pick songs that fill your body with joy —if you find yourself shimmying in your seat, you know it'll be a winner during your next workout.

CLASSIC ADRENALINE-PUMPING HITS

- "Shake Your Body," the Jackson 5

- "Another One Bites the Dust," Queen

- "Runnin' Down a Dream," Tom Petty

- "Instant Karma!," John Lennon

- "Should I Stay or Should I Go," the Clash

- "Black Dog," Led Zeppelin

- "Welcome to the Jungle," Guns N' Roses

- "Let's Dance," David Bowie

Day 22

Choose a special time—a road trip, your wedding, your child's first year—and start sorting through your digital library or box of snapshots, recalling the fun moments. Scientists say positive memories greatly enhance our present happiness and can even reduce depression. So pick the images you love, the ones that tell the story of this experience, and assemble them into a book you can flip through again and again.

GO THE EXTRA MILE

Looking at photos with children—your own kids, nieces and nephews, dear friends—sparks conversations about the past, which strengthens relationships and makes you happier.

MAKE a PHOTO ALBUM

DO A METTA MEDITA-TION

Day 23

According to legend, a group of monks once returned early from a spiritual quest for fear of evil spirits in the forest. Upon hearing this, Buddha taught them a metta (loving-kindness) meditation:

May I be happy
May I be well
May I be free from suffering
May I be peaceful and at ease

First recite while directing the sentiments inward; then repeat while thinking of someone you love, someone you feel neutral about, someone you find challenging, and finally someone you don't know. This practice gave the monks courage to return to their quest, where they found more welcoming spirits awaiting them. May it do the same for you!

SCHE
DULE@
CHECK
UP ✓

Day 24

It goes without saying that good health
and happiness are linked. So it's no
surprise, psychologists say, that when
we ignore our body's basic needs, we
compromise our abilities to manage
moods and cope with daily stressors.
In other words, call today to make an
appointment with that doctor you've
been meaning to see. You'll feel
better already.

Day 25

Ready, set . . . don't go. Instead, spend the next twenty-four hours recharging body and soul in the headquarters of your heart. We all need to check in with ourselves from time to time, and where better than your own personal sanctuary? Stay in your pj's or walk around naked, cook a meal or call for delivery, reorganize the closet or watch a movie in bed—this is your mental health day to do with as you wish.

SPEND THE DAY @ HOME

Day 26

Life can be hard and the world can be scary, but focusing on the negative only primes your brain to notice more negativity. Happily, you are in control. Escape the cycle of pessimism and sadness by choosing to keep an eye out for goodness and generosity. Positive thinking feeds itself the same way that negative thinking does, so get the ball rolling and it will get easier and easier to find little things to be happy about. Today, keep track of all the kind interactions you witness—as the list grows, so will your optimism and faith in humanity.

LISTEN TO A PODCAST

Day 27

Here's a way to fill your head with positivity: Browse iTunes for podcasts about your passions and interests. Your headphones are a ticket to greater connections—whether you are on your commute or on your couch. Our media diet has a great impact on our well-being, and study after study shows that negative news consumption brings heightened stress. Balance out your listening. Choose topics and voices that educate, inspire, or transport—and hear the difference.

HOW TO LISTEN

Podcatcher apps make listening effortless by automatically updating the latest episodes. A few worth checking out: Downcast, Stitcher, Overcast, Castro, BeyondPod, and Podkicker.

A LITTLE "YOU-TIME"

Thoughts and actions that enhance mind, body, or spirit—what happiness researchers call "self-care"—are often surprisingly hard to manifest. Acts of self-care can range from the healthy (a short walk) to the indulgent (a bowl of ice cream), from the mental (a ten-minute meditation) to the physical (a spa mani-pedi). As much as anything, the key to meaningful self-care is intentionality—the purposeful investment of resources (money, time, emotion, effort) in our own well-being.

Studies show that when we regularly and consciously satisfy our needs, we benefit not only from the acts themselves but also from the thought patterns such acts reinforce. Self-esteem increases, stress decreases, and the brain's neural pathways literally reroute in ways that perpetuate self-affirming thoughts and self-improving behaviors. In short, the more we take care of ourselves, the more likely we are to continue to take care of ourselves. It is why, say, the occasional "unhealthy" treat—if framed as a kindness to oneself—can lead to a renewed commitment to, say, lifting weights (see page 138) or a mindfulness practice (see page 122). Decades of research have shown that when we invest in a project, we are far more likely to see it to completion. What better project to invest in than yourself?

Day 28

Clearing space in your cluttered schedule allows you to maximize your physical, emotional, and mental energy. Take a moment to assess if everything on today's calendar is really necessary. If a meeting is not linked to a specific objective and not something you really want to do, cancel it. It's that easy!

KEEP IT GOING

Experiment with something productivity strategists call "time blocking." Identify the chunk of time during the day when you work most effectively, and mark it as unavailable for others.

Day 29

Whether you're hitting high notes in the shower, channeling pop stars in the car, or sharing your booming baritone at karaoke night, singing powerfully and positively changes your brain. When you sing, musical vibrations move through your body, altering your physical and emotional landscape and reducing stress (cortisol) levels through the action of the endocrine system, which is linked to our sense of emotional well-being. Interestingly, group singing is the most transformative—research tells us that the benefits of belting out a song are enhanced when you are harmonizing.

Day 30

Boost a fellow human's mood/day/faith in people—all for the price of a coffee/movie ticket/toll—and watch how happy it makes you. Scientists found that this holds true from our earliest years. Toddlers experience greater happiness when giving away a treat than when receiving one. Adults too reported more pleasure after spending money on others.

An added impetus: Your generosity is contagious. Witnessing a random act of kindness inspires a domino effect, often resulting in the heartwarming stories of a thousand plus pay-it-forward chains at Starbucks and Tim Hortons.

PAY for THE PERSON BEHIND YOU

FIN-
ISH
SOME-
THING

Day 32

Write that memo, send that thank-you note, or take your winter coat to the dry cleaner. Whatever the task is that you've been putting off, it's time to cross it off your list and reap the psychological rewards. Knocking off a looming project frees the part of your consciousness that is (whether you know it or not) negatively obsessing over getting it done.

NOT SURE HOW TO START?

Break down the task into smaller parts. Start by simply opening a blank document, selecting a note card, or putting the coat by your front door.

Day 33

People often equate activism with anger, but advocating for an issue is actually a time-tested way to up personal happiness. Researchers from the University of Göttingen recently confirmed what Aristotle knew back around 330 B.C.: Those who take a political stand feel more alive and enriched, two important measures of well-being.

And you don't have to save the world to feel better. Take one small step—join a march, write a letter to your representative, sign a petition—and watch your mood rise.

AMPION
CAUSE

Day 34

Gather a needle, some thread, and an old T-shirt calling out for a new life and turn something that doesn't spark joy into a useful or beautiful piece. Focusing on a creative project puts you in a mindful flow; completing it provides a sense of accomplishment. Amazingly, that old T-shirt is now a tote bag you proudly carry on your shoulder.

CLOSE ENCOUNTERS

The research is overwhelming: The greater the number of meaningful relationships in our lives, the more likely we are to be happier. This is true for introverts and extroverts alike; everyone benefits from strong family ties, deep friendships, regular neighborly contact, and collegial workplace interactions. Indeed, studies show that people who routinely experience meaningful connection are less likely to suffer from maladies ranging from depression to the common cold and are more likely to sleep well, eat healthily, have high self-esteem, and live longer. The reason is largely physiological. Because humans evolved to be social creatures—depending on one another for survival—the human brain and body have been programmed to respond well to positive interaction, producing chemicals that lower stress levels, regulate appetite, and otherwise put people at ease.

There are numerous mental benefits from social connection as well, not least the fact that those who know us well are better suited to help solve our problems. Interactions that go beyond small talk also stimulate our brains, helping us to think more clearly and understand others better. This in turn decreases our chances of misreading behavioral signals, which often leads to conflict. And it's worth noting that what may seem like sadness is often just loneliness.

You'll notice that many of the challenges in this book involve reaching out in one way or another. That's because, sometimes, human touch is all it takes to brighten one's day.

APOLOGIZE

Day 35

There's no statute of limitations on healing old wounds. If something you did to someone is gnawing at you, reach out to that person today. To express true remorse, avoid being defensive ("but" should not be part of an apology), empathize with the person you hurt, offer your regrets, and ask what you can do to make it right.

Day 36

On the other side of the coin, research has found that forgiving someone—particularly someone we are close to––makes us happier. It also improves our health, decreases stress, and inspires us to be more benevolent. Still, forgiving is easier said than done when we are feeling wounded. But forgiving someone does not require reconciliation or the acceptance of bad behavior—it's something you do for yourself, not anyone else.

FURTHER READING

If you find grudges, resentment, and anger hard to let go of, explore the work of *Forgive for Good* author Dr. Frederic Luskin, who offers advice on cultivating the art of forgiveness.

MAKE a FASHION STATEMENT

Day 37

Want to feel like a million bucks?
Break out of your sartorial rut. Fashion
choices don't just change how we
look, they impact how we feel. British
psychologist Karen Pine asked a group
of students to wear Superman T-shirts
to test if doing so made them feel more
heroic. It did: Clad thusly, they rated
themselves more likeable as well as
physically stronger. Pine's suggestions
for happiness-inducing clothing include
playful or mismatched patterns, a
daring accessory, or anything else that
expresses your inner self and makes
you smile (which is also known to make
you happier—see Day 48).

Day 38

True happiness may lie within, but it helps to have someone leave a delightful card or package in your mailbox. Six days a week, through blizzards, pouring rain, and blazing heat, postal workers deliver for you (as do many others: sanitation workers, we're looking at you). If you don't have a chance to meet your mail carrier in person, leave a treat for him in the mailbox. Expressing gratitude helps us feel more—wait for it—grateful, which in turn draws our attention to the goodness and connectedness in the world. Life is, after all, a team sport.

USE FLOWER POWER

Day 39

A vase of tulips or peonies on your desk is an unexpected delight—and an easy way to add a touch of beauty to your daily grind. Blooms in the workplace have been shown to increase productivity, creative problem solving, and emotional well-being for both men and women, while reducing anxiety and stress. Those who woke up to flowers also reported a better mood, so consider getting two bouquets and placing one in your bedroom!

GO THE EXTRA MILE

Surprise someone with a bouquet of flowers, just because

Day 40

We often get the biggest reward from helping someone else. This is true both at work and in our personal lives. Mentoring crystallizes our own knowledge and sense of purpose, and doesn't require committing to a formal program. It's as easy as taking five minutes to explain how to improve a spreadsheet or an assignment or talking to a recent grad about her plans for the future.

BE@ MEN- TOR

Day 41

A movie ticket for one is the ultimate investment in me-time. Sure, it's a delight to choose the film, the perfect seat, and the snacks without any negotiation. But most valuably, going solo means your only concern is your own enjoyment. When we share an experience, a Harvard study found, our minds can't help but multitask as we (consciously or not) consider the other person's reaction. Today, focus on yourself.

GO THE EXTRA MILE

To provoke happy physiological responses in a lab, scientists show subjects movies in which the protagonist ends up—what else? —happy. Follow their lead and watch a feel-good flick!

Day 42

Therapists often suggest that kids who are feeling angry play catch to release their emotions and let off steam. Calm *your* inner child by grabbing a friend and a couple of mitts (or a football) and heading outside. The soothing repetition of the game, the steadying *thwap!* as the ball hits the glove, the safe intimacy of being together but standing apart—eyes, mind, and arms focused solely on making the connection—is a winning way to clear your head.

A LESSON LEARNED

A school of thought for those seeking greater happiness: Devote more time to education. This does not mean you must enroll in a formal institution; rather, expose yourself to a new subject or go deeper into a familiar one. This new knowledge may take almost any form: a useful painting technique or a new stew recipe, the history of your neighborhood or a more scenic route to work, a challenging yoga pose or the definition of an unfamiliar word. Whatever the scope or focus, the process of purposefully acquiring new expertise or skills will almost assuredly make you happier, in the moment and over time. That's especially true if the knowledge gained helps to meet a pressing need—whether it be a simpler method for sanding floors, a faster process for scrapbooking, or a better way to figure out the workings of the latest social media app.

The greatest benefit to learning any new skill comes when you have gained proficiency at or mastery of it. The human brain rewards the acquisition of expertise: As we learn, our brains produce happiness-inducing chemicals that govern a feedback loop that encourages us to continue to learn and improve. In fact, much like taking opioids and similar drugs, the process of gaining proficiency can be habit-forming, causing us to crave more such feelings. As addictions go, I can't imagine a better one.

SIGN UP FOR @ Class

Day 43

Today, indulge that life-affirming
desire to learn and improve your
mind. Wouldn't it be wonderful to
know how to blow a glass vase or sail
a boat or speak Spanish or play guitar
or properly cut veggies? Browse the
continuing ed catalogs of nearby (or
online) universities, see what piques
your interest, and put your name on
next semester's roster. Or search the
Internet for a class on that skill you
keep meaning to master—and
get excited to master it.

**POPULAR SITES TO
GET YOU STARTED**

- Coursera
- Duolingo
- edX
- iTunes U
- Khan Academy
- Skillshare

Day 45

It turns out that for many of us, the most delightful part of our vacation happens before we even take off: A Dutch study found that people were happiest in the eight weeks leading up to their getaway! One way to maximize pre-travel bliss is to plan several small trips. So grab a map, pick a spot, book a hotel, and start researching. Immersing yourself in the destination before you go offers another boost. Learning—and, more important, dreaming—about the restaurants, attractions, and neighborhoods you'll visit on your trip will enhance your experience when you actually arrive.

PLAN @ ROAD TRIP

DOWN UPSIDE WORLD YOUR TURN

Day 46

Try doing a handstand on a flat, grassy spot. Defying gravity will send a rush of blood to your head, which stimulates your brain and pituitary and hypothalamus glands to produce more happy-making and nerve-calming hormones. (Also, it's fun.)

If that proves too challenging, do this metaphorically by shaking up a daily habit. One easy example: Hold your fork and knife in the opposite hands while you eat.

ASK ABOUT THE good OL' DAYS

Day 47

The story itself will be worth the time, sure, but you'll also benefit from being in the presence of an older person. Studies show that as people age, they clarify priorities, appreciate the little things, focus on satisfying relationships, and are generally more trusting. All this leads to a more positive day-to-day existence, and less worry and anger. So in addition to a great tale, you'll get a firsthand look at the keys to a happier existence.

GO THE EXTRA MILE

Nursing homes are full of people who rarely get visitors. Stop by one in your neighborhood for a quick dose of perspective and gratitude.

Day 48

There are moments when the road to happiness requires each and every one of us to fake it 'til we make it. And as it happens, lightly biting a pencil with your front teeth for a minute or so during a rough spot in your day is a fantastic way to trick your brain into thinking that you're happier than you are. Why? Science! Holding your facial muscles just so will turn your expression into an approximate smile, and a smile—real or induced—has the marvelous ability to relax your chemical stress responses. When the corners of your mouth turn up, your body releases the feel-good trifecta of dopamine, endorphins, and serotonin, which has the added bonus of lowering your heart rate and blood pressure.

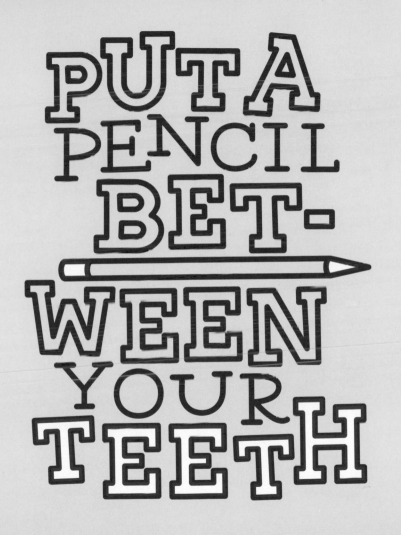

START FILLING YOUR PIGGY BANK

Day 49

It's easy to imagine how saving money
today will make you happy down the
road, once you've amassed a nice nest
egg. But there's a trick to delighting
in the clink of the coins the moment
you drop that fifty cents in your jar:
Give your stockpile a purpose—a trip,
a wedding, a new house—and indulge
those daydreams right then and there.
The anticipatory joy might make you
just as happy as the real thing.

MINDFUL MATTERS

Life can seem unbearably chaotic, one long losing effort to juggle dozens of simultaneous obligations, requests, and challenges. It's why even the idea of momentary stillness—any temporary respite from the onslaught of distractions—seems so appealing. Fortunately, there's a practical way to achieve this contained state of calm. The term for this mental magic is "mindfulness," which you have doubtless heard as interest in the practice continues to blossom. In essence, mindfulness is the act of narrowing your focus to a single thing—your breathing, a pleasing mental image, a beautiful physical item—for a brief time, gently steering attention back when it invariably wanders. Even two minutes of the practice can be transformative (see the following pages to learn how).

Mindfulness has its origins in Buddhism, which emphasizes awareness of the here and now over what has happened in the past or may happen in the future. A deep trove of research confirms that cultivating peaceful focus has short- and long-term physical and psychological happiness-related benefits: less stress, greater immunity to disease, lower levels of anxiety, and decreased incidences of depression. Studies have shown that mindfulness also correlates strongly with higher levels of self-compassion, likely because mindfulness requires practitioners to notice and refocus their concentration without judgment, and thus trains them to be less critical of their imperfections.

Finally, mindfulness has been shown to align with personality traits—openness and agreeableness—that lead to more and more satisfying interactions with others. And given what we know of the profound benefits of social connection (see page 90), it follows that mindful people tend to be happier too.

BREA

Day 50

Place one hand on your belly. Inhale deeply through your nose for a count of five and let your breath fill your abdomen so that your hand rises. Exhale slowly through your mouth, also for a count of five, and watch your hand fall. In the quest for greater happiness, there is perhaps no more effective tool than a deep breath. Practicing deep breathing for even two minutes a day has a dramatic impact. It rewires the nervous system, slows one's heart rate, helps regulate emotions, and minimizes the fight-or-flight response. And it's always there for us, right under our nose.

Day 51

Going to bed at 10:00 p.m. might be ideal for our health, but everyone knows that all the fun stuff happens after midnight. Although skipping out on sleep isn't a good long-term habit, research has found that one sleepless night—*just one*—can actually spike levels of dopamine (the happy-making hormone), giving you a few hours of a second wind, that extra burst of energy you feel when you push past the desire to rest. So tonight, fight the urge to fall into bed and let that dopamine hit carry you through a night of dancing, talking with friends, exploring the city after dark, and whatever else makes you happy.

STAY UP ALL NIGHT

Day 52

Here's a recipe for joy: Prepare a
dish you've never made. Do it on a
day when you can luxuriate in the
creating. Following an unfamiliar
recipe will focus your mind—*Do I need
to add the butter and the egg at the same
time? How much vanilla?*—and quiet
racing thoughts. Culinary therapy
is so effective at nourishing the soul
that it's used to relieve depression in
several health clinics. And the payoff is
delicious: a home filled with wonderful
smells and a blueberry pie or hot bowl
of soup to savor.

GO THE EXTRA MILE

Deliver a homemade
dish to someone in need
of a pick-me-up.

Day 53

If you've ever uttered the words "just one more," you are not alone. A recent study found that nine out of ten viewers watched three or more episodes of the same show in one sitting. In general, watching television does not make people happier, but experts suggest that watching a favorite show with a partner can increase intimacy, communication, and, when it's a good comedy, laughs. So queue up your guilty pleasure on Netflix, cuddle on the couch, and stream away.

Day 54

Going to a concert combines two happiness-boosting heavy hitters—listening to music, which releases the neurotransmitter dopamine, and sharing a positive experience with others, which is a well-being powerhouse. Whether in the quiet of the philharmonic hall or the roar of the rock arena, the vibrations take over as you connect to your companions, the crowd, the musicians, and—through the transporting power of the melody and the beat—yourself. It's your ticket to pure bliss.

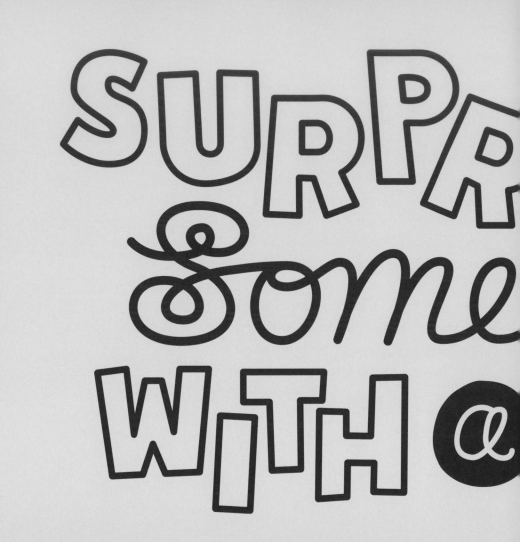

Day 55

Spark a domino effect of gratitude and joy. Gift giving activates your brain's pleasure and reward centers in the same way receiving a gift does, delivering a two-hour boost of warm, fuzzy endorphins, as well as hormones like oxytocin, which make you feel connected to others. Giving an unexpected gift has the added benefit of sidestepping the stress of finding the perfect present for a holiday or birthday and reminds everyone that it really is the thought that counts.

Day 56

Any club. Even being part of a group that meets only once a month produces the same happiness bump as doubling your income, according to *Bowling Alone* author Robert D. Putnam. It also cuts in half your chances of dying in the next year. As social creatures, we are wired for connections—that's how we have survived and thrived as a species. Now groups give us a greater sense of purpose and identity, and offer support in challenging times. Go find a community of folks who share your values or interests (books, religion, sports, or crafting, to name a few) and delight in their company.

KEEP IT GOING

Start a 100 Happy Days Club (we call it a "Happiness Circle") among friends or within your community to share and encourage each other on your happiness journeys. Get inspired at 100HappyDays.org /HappinessCircle.

PHYSICAL THERAPY

It may very well be impossible to overstate the connection between exercise and happiness. Literally hundreds of studies conducted around the world have shown that exercise eases depression, decreases stress, lifts mood, reduces anxiety, clears the mind, trains us to deal with adversity, and improves both body image and self-esteem. To be sure, some of this "exercise bounce" is a direct result of improved fitness. In general, healthier means happier, and that makes working out a particularly potent tonic. But studies suggest that the blessings physical activity bestows below the neck are secondary to those reaped above it.

Most significantly, exercise triggers the brain to increase production of endorphins, chemicals that assist the transmission of signals between neurons. While much remains to be understood about endorphins and what they do, it is clear that their increased production makes us feel better all around. That's because endorphins work much like opioids in both legal and illegal drugs, blocking pain signals and producing euphoric feelings. (Despite what you might have heard, though, research suggests you can't really become addicted to working out.)

If it all doesn't yet sound too good to be true, there's more: While training long and hard is certainly commendable, studies show that most of the exercise bounce is achieved within the first twenty minutes or so of physical activity, be it a pulse-quickening walk, a heart-pounding run, or muscle-building weight lifting. And exercise in group settings is doubly valuable to mental health. Credit the benefits of social connection (see page 90), of course, but also the fact that the presence of other participants increases the likelihood that you'll come back for more. So call up a friend or two and take a hike.

TAKE THE STAIRS

Day 57

You have arrived at a fork in the road: the ease of an elevator ride or the labor of walking up stairs. The benefits of taking the stairs go beyond toning muscles, though doing so burns twice as many calories as brisk walking. The climb also offers a moment of mindfulness, especially if you climb slowly and purposefully. The exertion will help focus your mind on the task at hand, so other worries take a backseat. And when you reach the top and the endorphins flow and your deep breathing reminds you of the effortful journey, enjoy the satisfaction of accomplishment and the peace of mind that comes from putting your body to work.

Day 58

Who can resist the childlike pleasure of bending the rules and eating pancakes at night? A quick search of #brinner on social media shows it to be a very popular culinary trend. Perhaps it's because carotenoids, the antioxidants that give egg yolks their yellow hue, are associated with optimism. Or maybe it's the simplicity of preparing the meal—you can skip the effort of stewing meat and chopping vegetables and just whip up a two-minute omelet. Whatever the reason, tonight's menu will have you seeing things a little more sunny-side up.

EAT BREAK-FAST for DINNER

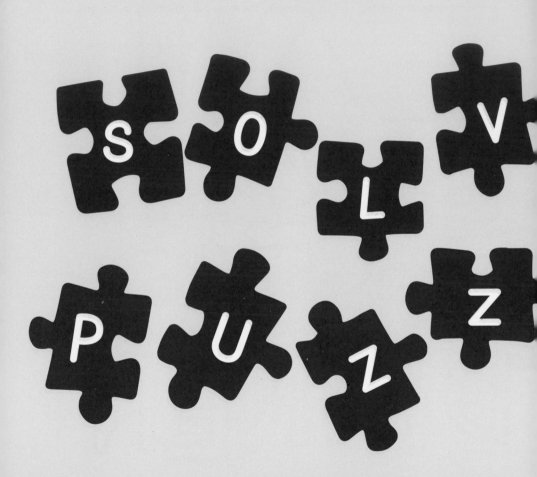

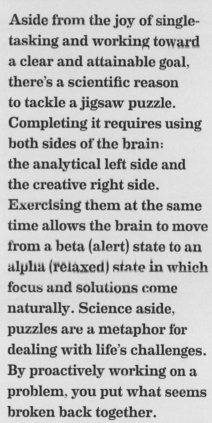

Day 59

Aside from the joy of single-tasking and working toward a clear and attainable goal, there's a scientific reason to tackle a jigsaw puzzle. Completing it requires using both sides of the brain: the analytical left side and the creative right side. Exercising them at the same time allows the brain to move from a beta (alert) state to an alpha (relaxed) state in which focus and solutions come naturally. Science aside, puzzles are a metaphor for dealing with life's challenges. By proactively working on a problem, you put what seems broken back together.

WATC

Viral V

Day 61

People who are chronically late are generally more optimistic—always expecting to beat the clock. But as the minutes tick away, the stress mounts. Today, give yourself the gift of an early arrival: Add a buffer to your travel-time estimate and say no to that one last thing you want to accomplish before heading out the door. Once you've arrived, appreciate the peaceful moment. Take a few deep breaths (see Day 50), read, people-watch—do anything but worry about getting to your destination on time.

Day 62

Yes, you can send a quick text—with emojis, even!—and communicate immediately, but then you'd be denying yourself the delight of picking out a perfect image, gathering a pen and your thoughts, writing just a few sentences, putting the card in the mail, and anticipating the recipient's delight when it arrives in her mailbox several days later.

GO THE EXTRA MILE

Sign up for our Pepmail program (100HappyDays .org/Pepmail), which connects people in need of cheering up with strangers happy to send them a handwritten note.

Day 63

Ha ha ha! Hee! Hee hee hee! In 1995, Indian family practitioner Dr. Madan Kataria started a movement called laughter yoga, and the giggling has since spread worldwide. Instead of jokes, Kataria offers a series of exercises in which you simply start laughing. In one, you chuckle while looking at an imaginary credit card bill in your hand; in another, you point your finger at someone, as if in an argument, and guffaw; a third has you raise your hands to the sky and silently belly laugh. Before you know it, the fake laughter turns real. Either way, laughing (whether "real" or "fake") leads to a host of benefits, including the release of those stress-reducing, happy-making chemicals that put you in a laughing mood.

PLANT HERBS

Day 64

Dirty hands, happy heart. Scientists say that keeping a home garden—whether in a few Mason jars on the windowsill or a plot in the front yard—is enormously beneficial to mood. For one thing, the act of gardening itself relieves daily stress and tension; for another, *Mycobacterium vaccae*, a harmless bacterium found in most soils, stimulates the release of happy-making serotonin.

GO THE EXTRA MILE

Get a double hit of happiness by planting aromatic herbs like lavender, rosemary, and lemon balm, whose scents have mood-lifting properties of their own.

THE CALL OF THE WILD

Recent studies have proved what many wise people—from the Greek philosopher Aristotle to your grandmother—have long known: The more time we spend in nature, the more likely we are to be happy. In one British experiment, more than eighteen thousand people participated in a challenge called "30 Days Wild," in which they gardened, stargazed, paddled down a river, walked in the woods, or swam in a lake every day for a month. Participants were later found to have experienced meaningful and sustained increases in health and happiness. The findings dovetail with earlier research demonstrating that sojourns in the great outdoors can ease anxiety and some symptoms of depression.

To some extent, nature's joyful powers are undoubtedly a result of the contrast it provides to most of our daily lives:

When researchers in Scotland monitored the brain activity of people taking walks in different parts of Edinburgh, brain-wave patterns of participants who walked in busy areas showed increases in both arousal and frustration compared with those of participants who strolled through parks, whose brain-wave readings indicated that they were calmer and more meditative. It makes sense: Poisonous plants and dangerous beasts aside, the natural world is a healthier world. An immersion into the sights, sounds, and smells of such an environment sends positive signals to our brains; one study revealed that people's moods rose just from entering a floral-scented room. Another study showed that most of the benefits of a nature-related activity occurred within the first five minutes. So what are you doing inside? Listen to Grandma and go outside and play!

Day 65

Night sky. Fresh air. Time to do
nothing but behold the wonder of the
universe. Few things will make you
feel as humble, hopeful, and heroic
all at once. Look up, just as when you
were a child, to admire the moon, spot
constellations, or search for a shooting
star. My astronomy kit includes a
lounge chair, a blanket, and a mug of
hot tea. What will be in yours?

Day 66

Early to bed, early to rise . . . as
Benjamin Franklin said, it really can
make you healthy, wealthy, and wise.
Plus, a good night's sleep will do wonders
for your mood. Lack of sleep makes
us anxious, worried, and pessimistic.
One study found that being even mildly
sleep deprived makes it harder to enjoy
good news. If you're waking up on the
wrong side of the bed, it's time to brush
up on your sleep hygiene. Avoid naps
and caffeine after noon, establish a
nice bedtime ritual like a warm bath or
meditation, make your bedroom quiet
and relaxing, and put away screens at
least an hour before you plan to doze
off. You'll wake up alert, refreshed, and
ready to take on the day with a smile.

RE-
CON-
NECT

Day 67

That teacher who set you on your path,
the childhood friend whose home was
your haven, the generous roommate
who didn't mind your mess, the old boss
who took a chance on you . . . there are
so many people who helped shape us
and for whom we feel forever grateful,
even if we are no longer in touch. Today,
friend one of them on Facebook, let him
know how much he meant to your life,
catch up on what's happened since you
last spoke, and fuel a happy trip down
memory lane.

Day 68

Above the door to the library of Thebes, the ancient Greeks inscribed the words "House of Healing for the Soul." Ponder this as you browse a bookstore today, exploring which subjects and titles lift your spirits. With that exciting new book in hand, find a quiet café in which to indulge your mind. Psychologist Victor Nell found that voracious fiction readers enter a type of hypnotic trance or dreamlike state in which everything slows as they read. Focus shifts away from the self, which is probably why a University of Liverpool study discovered that stress levels decreased by up to 68 percent after only six minutes of reading.

GO THE EXTRA MILE

Leave a favorite book—with a note of recommendation—in a park or café to be found by a stranger.

GET LOST in BOOKS

ASK for HE

Day 69

There are several suggestions for how you can help others throughout this happiness challenge. But today is your day to be on the receiving end. This is not always as easy as it seems, since asking for help can make us feel vulnerable and frightened. Author Brené Brown calls our societal desire to go it alone "one of the greatest barriers to connection." By making a request and accepting assistance, you build trust and intimacy and deepen relationships. When we share our burdens, we feel less isolated in the struggle and better about the world—and that helps everyone.

Day 70

"The way to begin is to begin."
—Eleanor Roosevelt

In a harried moment, focus on
one simple task to stop your mind
from spinning stories of paralyzing
impossibility. If you have a pile of dirty
dishes in your sink, start by washing a
single bowl. Focus on the feeling of the
water on your hands, the smell of the
soap, the smooth surface of the bowl.
Just as you carefully wash each dish
one by one, so too can you tackle any
other challenge you're faced with today.

ZEN AND THE ART OF MENTAL MAINTENANCE

Readers familiar with Buddhism will recognize the term "detachment" (or maybe "nonattachment" or "renunciation," alternate versions of the same idea). Detachment is the practice of letting go, and it has been shown to contribute mightily to individual happiness. It's a somewhat fuzzy concept, though, if only because it can mean different things to different people. For some, letting go is about forgiveness, laying aside anger, grudges, and resentments for no other reason than that they're anchors that prevent us from moving forward. (One of my favorite aphorisms: "Holding a grudge is like drinking poison and hoping another person will die.") For other people, letting go is about relinquishing control, allowing events to unfold as they may without any attempt on our part to steer them. For still others, letting go is about acceptance, abandoning the expectations we have for ourselves and others. But here's the beautiful part about detachment: however you understand it, getting better at it will make you happier.

Offering forgiveness, for example, has been shown to improve mood, self-esteem, and—not surprisingly—the quality of personal relationships. Likewise, people who see their life outcomes as equally balanced between aspects under their control and those dependent on external factors tend to be happier than individuals who believe they can determine most outcomes themselves. Researchers have also shown that lowered expectations raise happiness, in part because nice surprises are smile stimulators but also because the absence of disappointment means we're less likely to experience stress, sadness, anger, and various other happiness-reducing physical states or emotions. Letting go, in other words, is actually a way to grab more joy.

Day 71

Take a moment to practice the Japanese philosophy of wabi-sabi, finding beauty in broken, old, and imperfect things. Release yourself from the pressure to be perfect by smashing something on purpose.

. . . And then, if you're handy, put it back together again, *kintsugi*-style. *Kintsugi*, the Japanese practice of repairing objects with lacquer mixed with gold or silver to highlight (rather than hide) cracks and imperfections, is an art that reminds us that life is a beautiful journey—even when things get messy.

Day 72

A bookshelf. A model airplane. A tree house. Whatever the undertaking, few idylls are more satisfying than one spent building a real-life, honest-to-goodness useful thing of beauty. The gratification is as much about the road as the destination. With every sweaty blow of a hammer and labored turn of a screwdriver, you'll create a refuge for yourself from the ordinary pulse of life, losing track of time as your creation comes to life. This is deep focus, a chance to surrender to tactile work done with your own two hands. And it's a light that glows long after, a source of mellow I-built-that pride each time you glance at the new bookshelf in the hallway, the model airplane on your office desk, or the tree house in the backyard.

DO A HAND MUDRA

Day 73

Dating back to centuries-old Hindu and Buddhist ritual, mudras can shift your energy—and can be employed wherever and whenever. The power of these sacred gestures is in the fingers, each of which represents one of the five elements in the universe and our bodies: fire (thumb), air (index finger), ether (middle finger), earth (ring finger), and water (pinky). Holding them in various positions—aka "seals"—for even a few minutes stimulates healing and aligns imbalances. There are 108 postures from which to choose; the Ksepana mudra included here is as soothing to the soul as it is simple to master.

KSEPANA MUDRA

Interlace all but the index fingers, which should be straight and pressed together. When sitting, index fingers should point to the ground; when lying down, point index fingers to feet. Hold for two minutes while focusing on your exhale.

Day 74

PAM
your

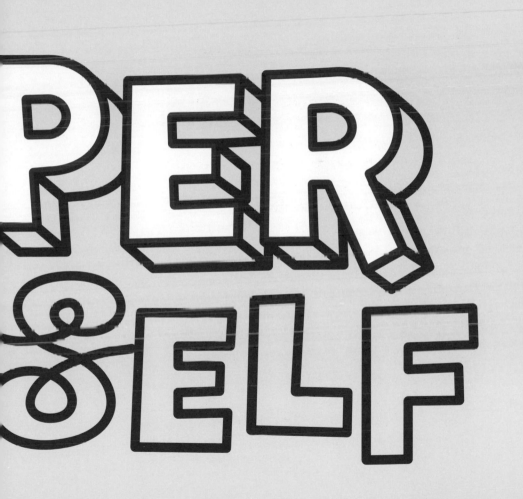

Day 75

Study after study has shown that quality relationships are the best way to increase well-being. Developing lasting friendships—the kind that will make you happier—takes effort (just like your exercise or healthy-eating habit). So that cool person you really like but haven't gotten to know, the one you met through a friend or at your kid's school? Call her up for an impromptu lunch date. You'll have a blast learning about each other's childhood or hobbies and discovering what you have in common over a plate of pasta or a glass of wine—and afterward, reflecting on the fun of forging a connection. And then when your new friend texts to set up another meeting, you'll feel happy all over again.

Day 76

Head outside, put one foot in front of the other, and when you come to a fork in the road, let your interest and instinct guide your direction. Notice the beauty of the trees, the color of the sky, the faces of passersby, the barking dogs, the architectural details, the signs, the storefronts, and, as you go farther, the tiredness of your legs and the calm of your mind.

GO THE EXTRA MILE

Scientists say happy people walk with an upright, steady torso and swinging arms. Give it a try—or invent your own version of a "happy walk" and take it for a spin!

Day 77

"For it is in giving that we receive."
—Francis of Assisi

Think of generosity as a practice, similar to mindfulness or gratitude, to be cultivated within yourself on this quest for greater happiness. The last piece of cake, a seat on the subway, an extra-large tip, and the benefit of the doubt are all ways to sate another human's hunger for kindness and help your spirits to soar.

OFFER up THE LAST piece

CUD-DLE @ PET

Day 78

For a dose of love, warmth, and connection, it's hard to beat playing with a puppy or listening to a cat purr. A recent study found that petting a dog or cat for even three minutes has the same mood-boosting effect that cradling a baby does for its mother. In each circumstance, the body releases oxytocin, aka the "cuddle hormone," which triggers happiness, relaxation, and increased trust.

NO PET AT HOME?

Spend time with a friend's pooch or volunteer at an animal shelter.

TAKING CONTROL

Elsewhere in this book I explain the benefits of detachment, the Buddhist practice of letting go that is a reliable method to gaining greater happiness and contentment (see page 170). But there's a flip side to this state of being—exercising control over one's life—and it has benefits too, not the least of which is the satisfaction that comes from what one team of social scientists described as "the ability to override or change one's inner responses." These researchers were, of course, talking about self-control. This concept refers less to acts of willpower—not eating that cookie or making sure to work out every day—and more about self-determination, small acts of sovereignty that make you feel your life is your own. That's one reason people are generally happier in old age: they are less concerned with what others think. Instead, they are motivated more by their own desires than by external forces.

GET TO WORK

The greater our sense of self-determination—our ability to decide what we will or won't do, whether the action is minor, such as saying no to a party invitation (see Day 94), or life-changing, such as retiring—the more likely we are to be happy. Indeed, in one study of retirees, scientists sought to measure the happiness of people who retired gradually versus those who stopped working cold turkey. What the researchers found was that the pace of retirement was not especially relevant, but it mattered a great deal whether study participants believed they controlled the process themselves. The greater this sense, the greater the retirees' reported happiness. To be sure, controlling one's daily activity and long-term destiny involves compromise, and not only because happy-making social connections require them. That said, people in general should spend more time doing what they want. Especially if what they want is happiness.

Day 79

Today, devote time and effort to a project or pursuit—something that really matters to you and matches your abilities. When we are engaged in something that is both meaningful and suitable, we become happier and healthier, says Cambridge University psychologist Brian R. Little. So go advocate for a cause or train for a 5K or learn to fish . . . whatever feels central to your passions and values.

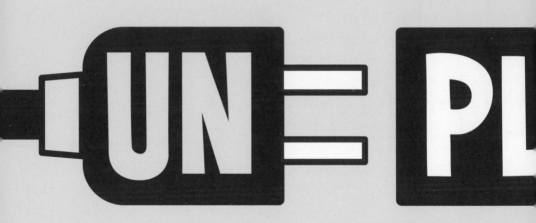

Day 80

Technology is wonderful, allowing us to connect, create, and learn in ways previously unimaginable. But it's not everything. And most of us are too tethered to our tech, checking e-mail constantly and even sleeping with our smartphones. Today, see what it feels like to power down and take a break from the screen. Start in the morning—savor that first cup of coffee or a long shower before logging on. Go for a walk with a friend, take your child out for lunch, or treat yourself to some unwired me-time and leave the device at home. Free yourself from distracting pings or notifications. And tonight, close your computer an hour before bedtime. It will improve your sleep, and your mood tomorrow too.

PAY A COMPLIMENT

Day 81

We all know how nice it feels to be congratulated on our hard work, killer fashion sense, or beautiful singing voice. But research shows that compliments bring *both* parties joy, on the giving and receiving end. So today when you notice something wonderful about another person, share the love and keep the positive vibes flowing.

GO THE EXTRA MILE

Write compliments on sticky notes and leave them for strangers to find on a park bench, telephone pole, or bathroom mirror.

Day 82

Originally used in Hinduism to focus meditative practice, mantras are a simple way to find inner calm in even the most trying of times. Repeating short, simple words or phrases—"Om," "I am," and "I choose happiness" are just a few examples—can help you tune out the negativity and reorient your mood while walking, meditating, driving, working, cooking . . .

Say them aloud or in your head whenever and wherever the desire strikes, and as many times as you find soothing.

BRER
HAB

Day 83

Bite your nails? Gossip a bit too much? Obviously the things we do that we wish we didn't can impede our happiness, health, and social relationships. Quitting will have immediate rewards (maybe you'll end up with nicer nails, more close friends, etc.), and proving you can stick to a positive change will help you feel better overall too. But no need to get ahead of yourself—research suggests that even attempting to stop can make you feel better, so delight in that first step today.

VOLUN-
TEER

Day 84

Charitable organizations usually ask for money, but time and effort are equally effective and precious resources to give away. And rare is the online financial donation that can mimic the visceral and spiritual joy linked with showing up and serving. The cause can and should be dear to your heart—soup kitchen, elder visit, community garden, political campaign, or literacy program, to name a handful—but the effect of simply being there in person is itself enriching. You'll create human connections that nourish the soul and come away with a greater understanding of your community or world, and those who live in it.

A NOTE OF THANKS

It will surprise few readers that one "secret" to happiness is being thankful for life's bounties, large and small. In fact, what might be called a "gratitude movement" has reached most corners of the globe. And far from just another passing trend on social media, the power of gratitude is supported by a wealth of research. Dozens of studies have demonstrated that grateful mind-sets and practices increase happiness, and for a variety of reasons. For example, being grateful focuses us on life's positives, which often go unnoticed amid hectic periods, and the more time we spend thinking about the good, the less time we have to ruminate on the bad. Additionally, noticing our good fortune—especially that which derives from the kindness of others—encourages us to perform unselfish acts of our own (see page 42). It has also been shown that taking the time to count your blessings boosts self-esteem, likely the result of some nonconscious logic: *Others value me enough to bestow these favors, so I must be a worthwhile person.*

Whatever the underlying reasons, the causal line from gratitude to happiness is undisputed. In one well-known study, researchers asked three groups to write a few sentences each week, the first group on reasons for being grateful, the second on annoyances or other sources of displeasure, and the third on the events of their day, with no thought to their positive or negative overtones. After two and a half months, those asked to focus on gratitude were not only more optimistic and positive about their circumstances, they also exercised more and had fewer doctor visits. So there's one more reason to develop a gratitude practice: It is sure to provide you with even more reasons to be grateful.

Day 85

Sure, we say thank you to the gate agent who went the extra mile to get us home in a family emergency, the customer-service rep who patiently talked us through every line item on our phone bill, the barista at our regular coffee place who hands us a latte before we've placed our order. But today, amp up that praise with a specific mention in an online review or a note to his or her manager or a company higher-up. Spreading the love—especially when it's well deserved—makes our own hearts swell too.

Day 86

Open a document on your computer or grab a pen and paper and start writing. Spend the next twenty minutes putting down whatever is in your head, paying no attention to grammar or punctuation. No one will ever see this, so feel free to write about your relationships, your childhood, your secrets, your worries, and your emotions. Throughout forty years of research, psychologist James W. Pennebaker has found that this exercise leaves people feeling both happier and healthier.

KEEP IT GOING

Pennebaker recommends doing the twenty-minute writing exercise for at least three days in a row.

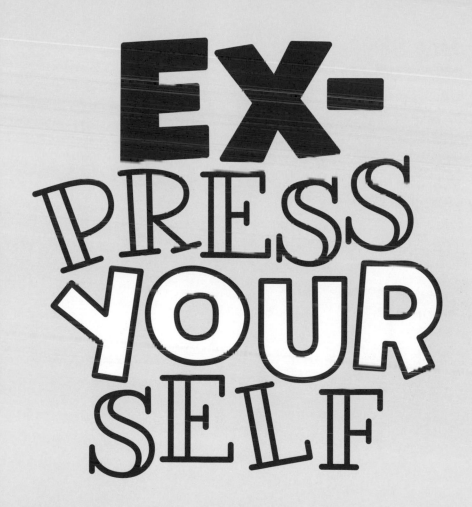

Funny
FRIEND

Day 88

Everybody has a spot for all the junk in their house that has no real home. The problem is, muddle and mess are linked to psychological stress. Do yourself a favor and spend an hour or two sorting through the crammed-in chaos. Find a place right away for the few things you actually need, and dump all the rest. Then open up that drawer and admire the calming beauty of your work.

RIDE A ROLLER COASTER

Day 89

The rickety sound of the wheels
climbing higher and higher, your
whitening knuckles as you hang on for
dear life, a mix of "Here we go!" and
"Why did I do this?" in your stomach.
The only way out is through—or rather,
down and around and around again.
Hair flying, eyes wide, mouth open,
screams you didn't know you could
scream. Terrifying-but-safe experiences
like these allow us to revel in our
vitality. Scientifically speaking, you'll
get a shot of adrenaline and endorphins,
leaving you feeling quite high when you
are back on solid ground. What a thrill.

Day 90

A happiness trifecta: water, greenery, and small animals. Experienced on their own, each has the ability to lift your mood and soothe stress. But today you get to experience the rejuvenating power of all three, and it's as close as the nearest duck pond. Grab a handful of oats (bread is actually harmful to birds!) and head out. The ducks will appreciate the treat, and you'll appreciate the beauty of nature's diverse offerings.

Day 91

It seems counterintuitive, but minor-key tunes actually offer a major lift. Researchers discovered that listening to sad songs evokes feelings of empathy, wonder, and nostalgia—and sparks our imagination. In those moments when we feel most blue, sorrowful tunes offer consolation and comfort, which then make us feel so much better. So queue up Adele or Hank Williams and give yourself over to the feelings.

GO THE EXTRA MILE

Curate a comforting playlist for a friend who is feeling blue.

FAKE IT 'TIL YOU MAKE IT

When all else fails, smile. This is my final advice to you, fellow happiness seeker. As you strive to find joy among the countervailing challenges of the everyday, sometimes you just have to put the cart before the horse. In their insightful book *The Wisest One in the Room*, the psychologists Thomas Gilovich and Lee Ross include a chapter titled "The Primacy of Behavior." Their thesis, supported by decades of research, suggests that we can use our bodies to trick our brains into thinking we're feeling a particular emotion, which actually makes us experience that emotion. This ability of bodies to influence emotions is why motivational speakers such as Tony Robbins encourage people to clap their hands rapidly before making a public appearance; the resulting adrenaline and endorphin rush mimics the physical experience of success and pleasure, doubtless improving the performer's mind-set. So smile when you're not especially happy (see Day 18), raise a victorious "V" before an outcome is decided, or rub your hands together in gleeful anticipation when you're anxious. The best way to feel happy or positive or confident might just be to act that way first.

Strike A POWER POSE

Day 92

Sitting up straight—head upright, chest forward, shoulders pulled back—lifts more than your torso. Researchers have found that posture has an immediate, and noticeable, impact on mood. One study asked participants to assume the posture associated with confidence and doubt. (Confident individuals tend to take up a lot of room, while less confident people often cave in on themselves.) Wouldn't you know it: People who struck "power poses" experienced an increase in testosterone production and a drop in cortisol, a hormone associated with stress. So sit up straight and feel the smile cross your face.

Day 93

The simple fact that you are on this journey means you understand the unexpected delight of opening yourself up to more. Today is your day to explore what happens when you deliberately opt in. Say yes to that inconvenient meeting or random lunch, a crazy dare or silly prank, and whatever else comes your way today. Allow yourself the freedom to experiment. Give yourself permission not to worry. Who knows? You might just discover a spark of joy that lasts a lifetime.

Day 94

And just as essential to a happier you
is twenty-four hours to practice the art
of no. Today when someone asks you
to meet up or help out, pause first. Ask
yourself: Is this is something I want to
do with my precious time and energy?
If not, bravely and confidently decline.
Any momentary discomfort will soon
be replaced with a relaxed schedule, an
open heart, and a new state of mind, all
of which are yours to fill with whatever
you delight.

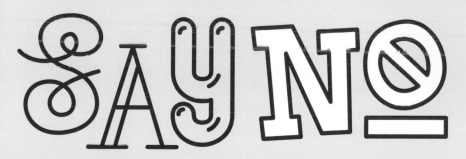

GET A massage

Day 95

Today, give yourself some TLC by addressing that knot in your shoulder, those exhausted feet, or the literal pain in your neck. Massage is a centuries-old practice, and lucky for us, we live in a world where a ten-minute back rub is only a nail salon away. It feels great, in part because touch activates the part of our brain that's linked to feelings of reward. It's powerful enough to help cancer patients cope with their pain and anxiety, and it will put a spring in your step too.

Day 96

"Eating food with your hands feeds not only the body but also the mind and the spirit."
—Ancient Vedic proverb

The fork didn't find its way onto most European tables until the nineteenth century, and some would argue that it's a shame it ever arrived. Today, ditch the utensils and grab a bite with your fingers. You'll be more likely to notice the meal's textures, colors, and aromas. The experience becomes much more sensory. That's why many people around the world still prefer using their hands to eat.

GO THE EXTRA MILE

Eat with your eyes closed. Shutting off your sight naturally shifts awareness to the other senses, heightening the experience of each bite.

START a TRA-
DITION

Day 97

Traditions provide us with a source of identity, solidify groups, and keep families close. In a fast-paced, ever-evolving world, they offer comfort and connection. It's very grounding to know what to expect. Here's the beautiful thing: You have the power to start new traditions, either to replace ones that don't bring joy or to augment those that do. Whether it's misfit Thanksgiving, Tuesday-night trivia, or opening day with the gang, you can choose how to mark a moment in time, and do it again and again until you can't imagine life without it.

BLOOD

Day 99

There is so much good in you. Today, put it down on paper as if you were expressing your admiration for a close friend or a lover: your best qualities, the things about yourself that make you proud, sweet memories, future dreams . . .

RULES TO WRITE BY

- This is only for you—no one needs to read what you wrote.

- You can keep it short or write pages and pages.

- Be gentle with yourself, keeping the thoughts positive and appreciative.

Day 100

As you now know, happiness is very personal. Only you can say what will truly bring you joy. Today, close your eyes, ask yourself what will offer delight in this very moment, and listen closely. Answer in hand, go forth and pursue it.

Then spread the love! Share your ideas for happier days with others on the journey with the hashtag #100HappyDaysBook.

AFTERWORD

You finished the #100HappyDays challenge! Congratulations!

Exploring what brings you joy for 100 days is an extraordinary feat. Much like a marathoner crossing the finish line or a world traveler who has made her way around the globe, you deserve to celebrate the completion of your journey. Whether that means giving yourself a pat on the back or throwing yourself a big party (whichever would bring you most happiness, of course!), I hope you'll take some time to revel in the accomplishment.

Why do I think it's so remarkable? Because most people are unaware of what makes their heart sing. Their days are filled with the routine and the expected. Not you, though. You swapped complaints for consciousness, and in doing so, learned that happiness is a choice. Your reward is a unique and beautiful perspective on life.

You may be wondering what's next. From my own experience, and from witnessing that of countless others, I suggest you think of happiness as a muscle. Yours is now quite strong, but it requires regular use, which is why the challenge is designed to build a happiness habit. Consider the marathoner. When the race is over, the passionate runner will continue logging miles in the days, weeks, and years to come. And just as most marathoners reflect on their race experience, so too should you consider the past 100 days. What made you light up? What didn't work? What was surprisingly wonderful? What reinforced things about yourself that you suspected deep down? Let these insights propel the new phase of your journey.

Practically speaking, some find it valuable to continue posting photos. Others move on to a gratitude journal. Many find it helpful to redo the challenge once a year. Better yet, encourage someone else to start the challenge, or establish a happiness club in your neighborhood. Use the gatherings to keep each other motivated or do something delightful from this book together. Tell us about your local clubs and experiences at Hello@100HappyDays.com. After all, we know that happiness is contagious.

No matter what follows, let this challenge be a reminder to you—and those around you—that happiness is possible in even the smallest moments. And that creating those moments every day adds up to a great deal of happiness.

THANK YOU

If there is one thing I've learned from doing the #100HappyDays challenge, it is how grateful I am for the people I have happened to meet in my life. From my closest friends to complete strangers, so many of them have been beyond supportive during the creation of this book that the list of names could easily fill another book entirely. To all of you, with all my heart, thank you!

Thank you to Artisan for publishing a #100HappyDays companion that readers can be proud to hold in their hands and return to again and again, in both good times and bad. Thank you to Bridget Monroe Itkin and Shoshana Gutmajer for their continual patience and boundless kindness while driving the process forward, as well as to the rest of the Artisan team: Lia Ronnen, Sibylle Kazeroid, Renata Di Biase, Nancy Murray, and Hanh Le. Without Leslie Koren and Gary Belsky from Elland Road Partners, my excited thoughts would have never been put into words so beautifully, and without the encouragement of Cait Hoyt from CAA, this journey might never have started.

And thank you to Timothy Goodman and John Sampson for bringing these pages to life.

Thank you to my alma mater, SSE Riga, for instilling in me the belief that nothing is impossible. Thank you to my SSE & HEC classmates, Sandbox Network, and my closest friends for showing me how many different paths there are to reaching the same goal: a better world. Thank you to the army of #100HappyDays "happiness ambassadors" who tirelessly spread the message and live by the values of the challenge every single day. Thank you to Valentina Pozzobon for the endless love that fills up my inner bucket and spills over to the world.

Finally, I am truly blessed to have parents like Valentina and Sergey Golubnichy. Their unconditional support gives wings to my dreams. Their ability to find joy in the ordinary, make the most out of what they have, and celebrate even the smallest of victories is one of the most precious gifts they could have ever given me. It is at the foundation of the challenge, this book, and me as a person. For that I am forever grateful.